WORLD PRESS PHOTO 1990

PHAIDON · OXFORD

PHAIDON UNIVERSE · NEW YO

The International Jury
at work. During an
action-packed week in
February, the nine-member
jury fulfilled
its tightly
scheduled task
on the top floor
of KLM's Head Office
just outside Amsterdam.
Photos: Peter Denkema

CONTENTS

The annual international competition comprises nine categories, which together cover the entire field of photojournalism. In every category three prizes are awarded for single photographs and three for picture stories. The first prize winners in each category are presented with the Golden Eye Trophy. From the winning photographs the International Jury selects:

In 1955 a number of Dutch press photographers launched the idea of organizing an annual international contest and exhibition of press photographs. Their initiative was enthusiastically received and resulted in the World Press Photo Holland Foundation.

This organisation, established in the Netherlands and led by Dutch nationals, has set itself the task, under the patronage of HRH Prince Bernhard of the Netherlands, of creating and stimulating a world-wide interest in press photography as an important means of promoting international understanding and the freedom of the press. Its principal activities are the organization of the annual international press photography contest, the presentation of the resulting exhibition in as many countries as possible, and the publication of this yearbook in several languages. In this task the Board of World Press Photo is assisted by committees in France, the United Kingdom and the United States, and by an International Advisory Board whose composition reflects a wide-ranging and professional interest in World Press Photo.

The Foundation operates as an independent, non-commercial cultural organisation, whose activities are financed by a subsidy from the city of Amsterdam, sponsorships from Eastman Kodak Inc. in Rochester USA and KLM Royal Dutch Airlines. The primary source of income, however, are the payments received for the annual exhibition. Details about charges and conditions are available from the Foundation's office in Amsterdam.

World Press Photo Foundation
Van Baerlestraat 146
1071 BE Amsterdam
The Netherlands
Phone +31(20)766-096
Fax +31(20)764-471
Telex 10611 aoc nl att. WPPh

The members of this year's Jury
from left to right:
Pedro Meyer, Mexico
Jens Schetelich, GDR
Michael Rand, UK (chairman)
Grazia Neri, Italy
Jean Dieuzaide, France
Raghu Rai, India
Sandra Eisert, USA
Gennady Koposov, USSR
Peter Martens, The Netherlands
Ruud Taal, secretary
Photo: Capital Press

For me it was an honour to be invited back after 12 years to serve as chairman of the jury. Things have changed.

Thanks to the ever growing reputation of World Press Photo as *the* international photographic contest there were a massive 11,043 entries from 1,280 photographers, representing 64 countries. Almost 60 per cent of the entries were in colour, which makes a fundamental difference compared to a decade ago. When dissenters argue that television images have taken over visual communication, these facts seem to prove otherwise. Agreed, TV news coverage is the prime and most immediate source of information, frequently exciting, often stimulating and sometimes memorable; but is is nevertheless pictures, some of which you see in this book, which stick in the mind's eye.

People say that the frozen frame from a video recording will replace the news photograph. Show me one that equals the power of thought and decision that goes into a great news photograph. The disciplines are as different as painting is to engraving.

The jury was very aware of the tumultuous events that happened through the latter half of 1989. The failed people's revolution in China, followed by the uprisings which changed the face of Eastern Europe dwarfed the other news events of the year, or so it seemed. It was when we sifted through the pictures that we were forcibly reminded of the tragedies, misery and, too rarely, the joy that happened in other places.

We had some spirited discussions as we went through the distillation process over six days of judging. The news pictures stood out strongly, but this was inevitable in such a year. It was surprising that we were unable to make awards for Sports Stories. No prizes either in the Humour category, perhaps the most difficult and self-conscious of subjects to be captured by the camera. Most disappointing was the Arts section, where we made no awards for single pictures. All of us in the profession who have a commitment to World Press Photo must encourage photographers in this field to enter their work. We know it is there, it would add much to the contest and to the subsequent travelling exhibitions.

It was not obvious to the jury that Charlie Cole's photograph *Of Flesh and Steel* would be chosen as the Press Photo of the Year. But it became the inevitable choice as we realised it symbolised the events of 1989. It is not violent, and yet the underlying threat is there. Taken with a long focus lens, it is not very sharp. It has the luck of the photographer being in the right place at the right time. What it does express in the most simple, direct and well organised way is the ordinary man standing up to the might of a repressive regime, an inspiration to others in subsequent protests throughout the world. It is a picture that will remain with us.

MICHAEL RAND,
Art Director and Managing Editor
Sunday Times Magazine,
London, England

**WORLD PRESS
PHOTO
OF THE YEAR**

**FIRST PRIZE
SPOT NEWS
SINGLES**

CHARLIE COLE
Newsweek,
New York, USA
9001

Charlie Cole was born in Texas in 1955. He developed a taste for travel at an early age. In 1980 he left the USA for Japan, where he worked as a photojournalist for several magazines. Since 1987 his work for *Newsweek* has taken him all over Asia. He was deeply affected by the experience of covering the events in China.

9001
Of Flesh and Steel. The title of the Photo of the Year, taken on June 4, says it all. When during the 'Beijing spring' hope turned to despair, a lone youth, armed only with his courage, faced down a column of tanks. He stopped the progress of the People's Liberation Army for several minutes, then climbed on the first tank and was finally taken away by his friends. This photograph and others like it brought home the unequal struggle of Tiananmen Square to a worldwide audience. Later identified as Wang Weilin, 19, the young man went missing, feared dead.

BUDAPEST AWARD

FIRST PRIZE STORIES

HONOURABLE MENTION SINGLES

ANTHONY SUAU
Black Star,
New York, USA
9002

Anthony Suau, winner of the 1988 Premier Award and the Pulitzer Feature Photography Prize, was born in Illinois in 1956. He was on the staff of *The Chicago Sun-Times* and *The Denver Post* before joining the Black Star agency in 1984. His coverage of the events in Eastern Europe appeared in *Time*, *National Geographic* and *US News and World Report*.

9002
In January East German leader Erich Honecker said he expected the Berlin wall to endure for another century. By November it had become an anachronism - and so had Honecker. Hundreds of thousands of East Germans fled their country by various routes, until the government decided on November 9 to allow free travel to the West.

Two days later the frustration that had been building up over nearly three decades was finally unleashed on the symbol of division that the wall had become. Above: At the Brandenburg Gate West Berliners wave flags at East German border guards. Overleaf, a West German strikes a blow for freedom.

**BUDAPEST
AWARD**

**FIRST PRIZE
STORIES**

**HONOURABLE
MENTION
SINGLES**

ANTHONY SUAU
Black Star,
New York, USA
9002

9002 (continued)
After hammering at the concrete throughout
the night West Germans attempt to climb on
the wall at dawn, but they are repulsed by
police with water-cannon. Yet still they
pound on until they have forced a breach.
Above, police take control of the hole in the
wall, at least for the time being.

**HONOURABLE
MENTION
SINGLES**

**STUART
FRANKLIN**
Magnum,
Paris, France
9003

PETER TURNLEY
Black Star,
New York, USA,
for Newsweek
9004

9003
In the early days of the student uprising, youngsters gathered in Tiananmen Square didn't let their enthusiasm be dampened by a sudden thunderstorm. Reporters compared the exuberant atmosphere in the square to that at the Woodstock pop festival.

9004
A Chinese dissident pleads with soldiers to join in the battle for democratic reform. For a time, as army convoys refused to fire on the demonstrators, the power of persuasion seemed stronger than tanks.

**THIRD PRIZE
STORIES**

**STUART
FRANKLIN**
Magnum,
Paris, France
9005

9005
The full story of 19-year-old Wang Weilin,
whose heroism came to symbolise the spirit
of the 'Beijing spring'. Pictured around noon
on June 4, he so impressed the commander
of a T69 tank that he was allowed to climb on
top of it. Weilin is believed to have been later
executed.

**HONOURABLE
MENTION
STORIES**

**JACQUES
LANGEVIN**
Sygma,
Paris, France
9006

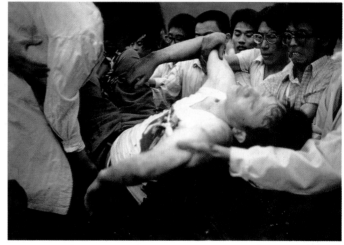

9006
During the first days of June it became apparent that the Chinese army intended to use all available means to repress the Beijing uprising. This picture story shows barricades being flattened, demonstrators rushing for cover, and casualties being transported by bicycle in the absence of ambulances.

ZONG HOI YI
Agence Vu,
Paris, France
9007

MICHAEL MACOR
The Tribune,
Oakland, USA
9008

9007
After a long night's riots and bloodshed the dawn of June 4 revealed this scene in the square in front of Tiananmen, the Gate of Heavenly Peace. The Beijing insurrection ended with bullets and burning. Identified only by his cap, this soldier was one of its many victims.

9008
A dramatic reminder of the proximity of the San Andreas Fault hit northern California on October 17. Measuring 7.1 on the Richter scale, an earthquake shook the area, wreaking havoc and claiming lives. This pick-up truck had been abandoned on the Cypress Structure Freeway.

HOWARD WALKER
Sunday Mirror,
Oldham, UK
9009

CINDY KARP
Black Star,
New York, USA
9010

9009
FC Liverpool fans are crushed against a fence at the Hillsborough football ground. On April 15, the opening of a gate at the English FA Cup semifinal against Nottingham Forest caused a stampede that left 95 supporters dead. More than half of them were under 30.

9010
While events in other parts of the world claimed the front page, photographers continued to risk their lives in El Salvador. The generation now growing up in this Central American country has never known lasting peace. Here a wounded soldier is carried from the battle zone.

**SECOND PRIZE
SINGLES**

RON HAVIV
AFP,
New York, USA,
for Time
9011

9011
'Sabotage by uninvited foreigners' was
officially the reason why General Noriega
declared the presidential elections of May 7
invalid. This much published picture of
opposition candidate Guillermo Ford
illustrates Noriega's idea of how to beat an
opponent. The general held on to power until
the end of the year.

SECOND PRIZE STORIES

CHRISTOPHER MORRIS
Black Star,
New York, USA,
for Time
9012

9012
By December General Noriega's days as president of Panama were numbered. The US reply to his declaration of war was Operation Just Cause. This sequence shows casualties of the 20,000-strong invasion, which ended in Noriega seeking asylum in the Vatican embassy.

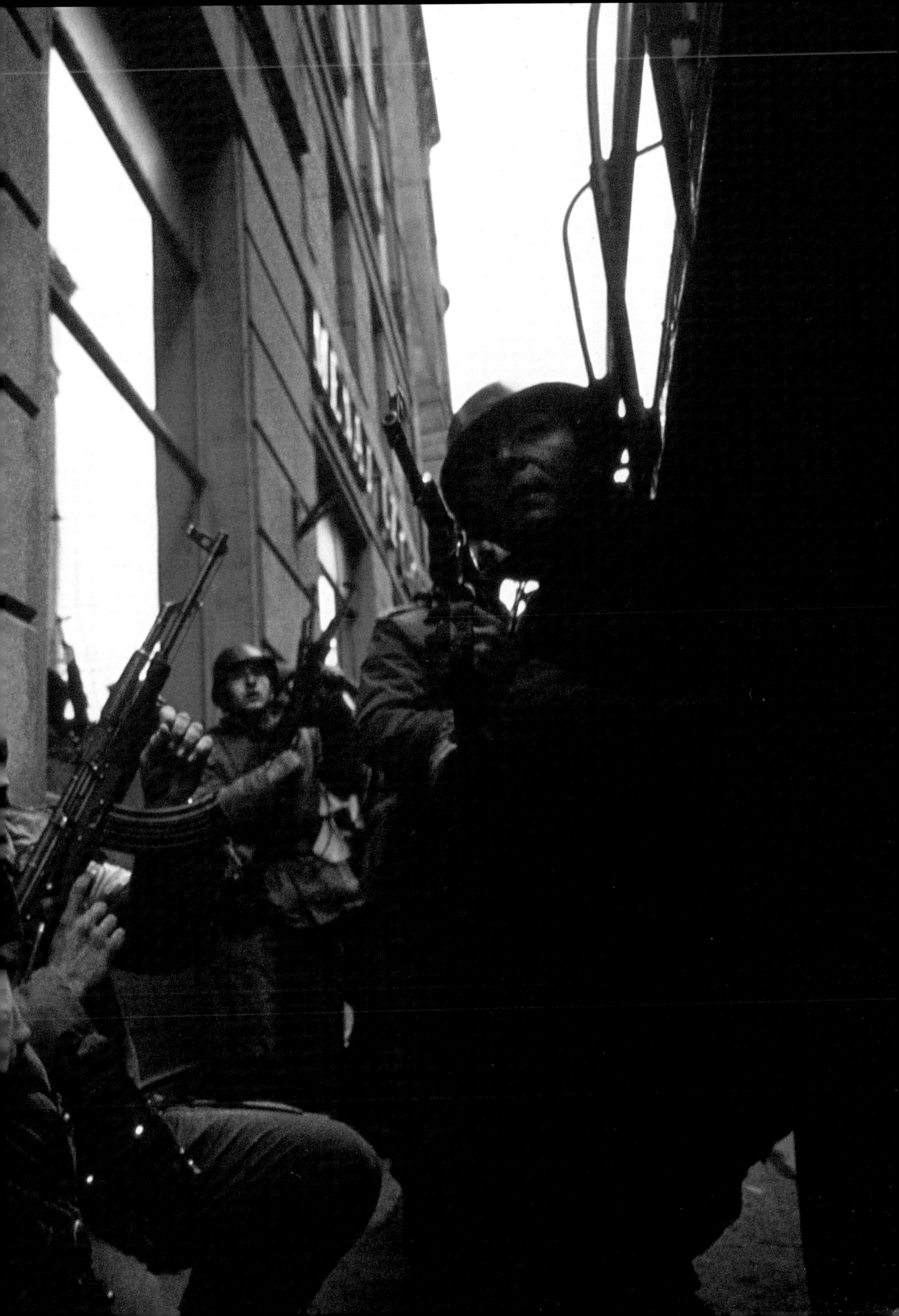

RIEN ZILVOLD
NRC/Handelsblad,
Rotterdam,
the Netherlands
9014

(previous pages)
**THIRD PRIZE
SINGLES**

**GILLES
SAUSSIER**
Gamma,
Paris, France
9013

9013
Timisoara, the name of the town where this photograph was taken, became a battle-cry of the Romanian revolution. For a long time it looked as if the tide of change sweeping over Eastern Europe would pass Romania by, but the arrest of a clergyman in Timisoara sparked off the first anti-communist riots.

9014
Christmas 1989 in Bucharest was anything but peaceful. Top: From Ceausescu's palace a soldier looks out on the burnt-out remains of the library building opposite. Bottom: Republic Square at 7.30 am on Christmas Day. Despite heavy fighting and the danger of snipers many civilians left the security of their homes.

HONOURABLE MENTION SINGLES

DAVID TURNLEY
Black Star,
New York, USA,
for Detroit Free Press
9015

9015
Start of a new era. Twenty-four years after
Nicolae Ceausescu established himself as
dictator, the army turned against him and
took over his office at the Communist Party
headquarters. Ceausescu and his wife
attempted to flee the country, but they were
subsequently arrested and executed.

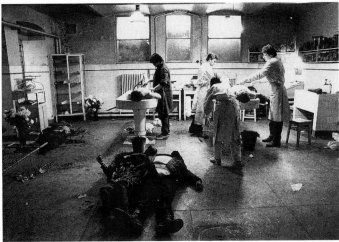

9016
Thousands of Romanians lost their lives during the turbulent days of December. Twenty-year-old Valentina Pandele (above right) was one of them. Soldiers and civilians joined forces against Securitate, Ceausescu's hated secret police.

OSKAR BARNACK AWARD

SECOND PRIZE STORIES

RAPHAEL GAILLARDE
Gamma,
Paris, France
9017

Raphael Gaillarde was born in Perpignan in southern France in 1948. He studied medicine and earned a living as karate teacher before he became a professional photographer. His work has been published in *Le Point*, *Le Figaro* and *l'Express*, and also in *Time* and *National Geographic* in the US. He has been under contract to Gamma since May 1989.

9017
This combination of a hot air dirigible and an inflatable raft enabled scientists in French Guyana to study various life forms on the roof of the rain forest at close range. Several international teams took part in the research, which encompassed insects, birds, tree frogs and vegetation (continued overleaf).

9017 (continued)
Above: The raft is lowered over the Amazon.
Once it is in position on the tree tops, a
researcher follows. Facing page: Having
found their footing, the scientists get to work
with their butterfly nets. Specimens captured
are carefully preserved.

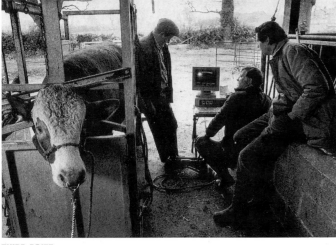

**THIRD PRIZE
STORIES**

**PATRICK
SUTHERLAND**
Norwich, UK
9018

9018
The destructive influence on the environment of modern farming methods prompted the photographer to make this reportage. Shot in Yorkshire and Norfolk, it was published in *The Independent Magazine*.

Facing page: Aerial crop spraying, and the demands made on a pedigree bull. Above: Sorting one-day-old chicks, a pesticide sprayer in protective clothing, and turkeys on their way to the table.

**FIRST PRIZE
STORIES**

**PHILIPPE
BOURSEILLER/
ARNAUD
DE WILDENBERG**
Sygma,
Paris, France
9019

9019
A team of two photographers recorded the Inlandsis expedition to Greenland. Above: The loneliness of the intrepid explorer, halfway up a wall of ice. Facing page clockwise from top: Passing through a cave of ice; flimsy shelters in the polar night; march back to camp in -15° C; descending into ever older ice masses.

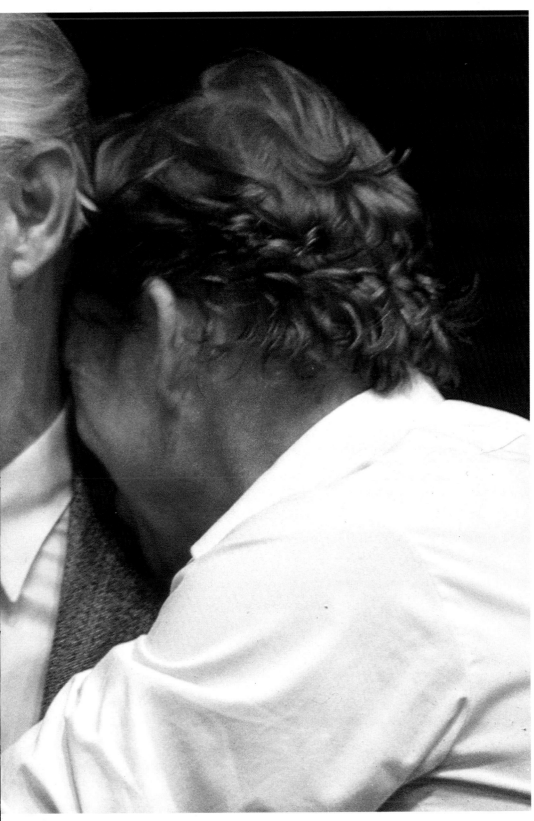

**FIRST PRIZE
STORIES**

**TOMAS
MUSCIONICO**
Contact Press Images,
New York, USA
9020

9020
In November it was Czechoslovakia's turn to
usher in a new era. Above, the two main
champions of change, Alexander Dubček and
Vaclav Havel, are shown in an emotional
embrace. The subject of this reportage is
human rights leader Havel, the playwright
who became president (continued overleaf).

A two-hour general strike Havel called for
November 27 was widely observed. The way
to the presidency lay open to the man who
shortly before had been called a 'nobody' by
Prime Minister Adamec. He appeared at
demonstrations and pop concerts (above).
Having been fitted with a new suit (facing
page), Havel was installed as president on
December 29.

**SECOND PRIZE
SINGLES**

**GEORGES
MERILLON**
Gamma,
Paris, France
9021

**THIRD PRIZE
SINGLES**

DAVID TURNLEY
Black Star,
New York, USA,
for Detroit
Free Press
9022

9021
At a Warsaw Pact meeting in Bucharest
Mikhail Gorbachev toasts his host,
Romania's long-time president Nicolae
Ceausescu. It was to be the last meeting
between the two Communist leaders.

9022
In a symbolic gesture, ex Czechoslovak
leader Alexander Dubček embraces the crowd
that has gathered in Prague's Wenceslas
Square. The man who tried to introduce
'socialism with a human face' in the spring of
1968 had to wait more than 20 years to see
his dream realised.

9023
Although the Communist Party continued to dominate Soviet politics, important changes were afoot. Dubbed 'man of the decade' by *Time Magazine*, Mikhail Gorbachev called elections for a new Congress of People's Deputies. He is shown surrounded by some of its 2,250 members.

9024
In Moscow's Red Square Boris Yeltsin is the focus of attention of his countrymen, who are eager to discuss the political situation. An immensely popular politician, Yeltsin was elected to represent Moscow in the new congress with almost 90 per cent of votes cast.

**SECOND PRIZE
STORIES**

**LEV
SHERSTENNIKOV**
Ogonyok,
Moscow, USSR
9025

9025

'We are all orphans,' said the editor of the Soviet magazine that published this series about Andrei Sakharov's death. 'The conscience of his country' was one of the titles given to this Nobel laureate, whose sincerity was valued by friend and foe. A brilliant physicist, Sakharov abandoned science to serve the cause of human rights.

In 1980 he was exiled to Gorky, but his return to Moscow in 1986 was triumphant. As a member of the new congress he continued to antagonise conservatives until his death, of a heart attack, at the age of 68. His grief-stricken wife Yelena Bonner (facing page) and hundreds of admirers accompanied him to his last resting-place.

CHRISTOPHER
MORRIS
Black Star,
New York, USA,
for Time
9026

PETER JORDAN
Network
Photographers,
London, UK
9027

9026
Two days after an attempted coup against his
regime has failed, General Noriega greets
supporters in the Panamanian town of
Santiago. The dictator lived to fight another
day, but was deposed a few months later.

9027
The Thatchers at home. A rare moment of
relaxation for British Prime Minister Margaret
Thatcher and her husband Denis. The couple
are pictured in their private apartment at no.
10 Downing Street.

SADDRI
DERRADJI
Montrouge,
France
9028

THIERRY
CHESNOT
Sipa,
Paris, France
9029

9028
The Dalai Lama, the spiritual and political leader of Tibet, against the dramatic backdrop of the Himalayas. A man of compromise and non-violence, the Dalai Lama was awarded the 1989 Nobel Peace Prize. The People's Republic of China, which has occupied Tibet since 1950, reacted furiously.

9029
On September 12, after the first free elections in an East Bloc country, Tadeusz Mazowiecki (centre) became Poland's new prime minister. Lech Walesa (right) continued to play an important role in the Solidarity-led coalition.

**SECOND PRIZE
STORIES**

**FRANÇOIS
PAOLINI**
Sygma,
Paris, France
9030

9030
As glasnost gains ground, reportages such as this one on juvenile delinquency give more insight into the Soviet penal system. Above, Tamara, who has been severely beaten up outside her home in a Moscow suburb, reports the incident to the police (continued overleaf).

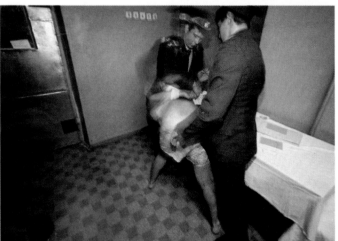

9030 (continued)
Stealing four car wheels is the crime for which Valeri (17, above right) has been sentenced to solitary confinement in a re-education camp. The photographs of an arrest and a body search were taken in Leningrad. Facing page: Public drunkenness is penalised according to strict rules, with heavy fines for repeat offenders. The fourth offence is punished with two years in a re-education camp. Shown with his wardens, 14-year-old Vitia (bottom left) is one of 72 detainees in Section 5 of the camp at Mouyask.

**FRANÇOIS
PAOLINI**
Sygma,
Paris, France
9031

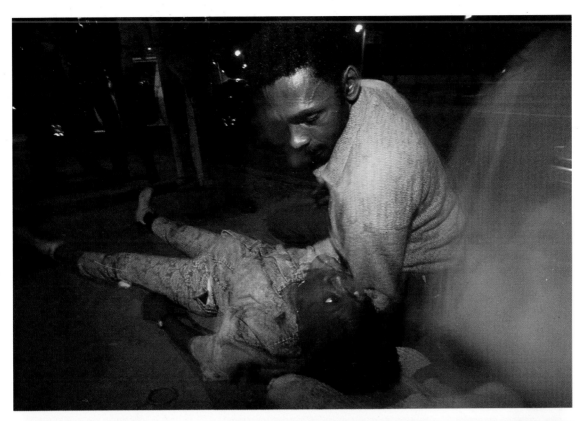

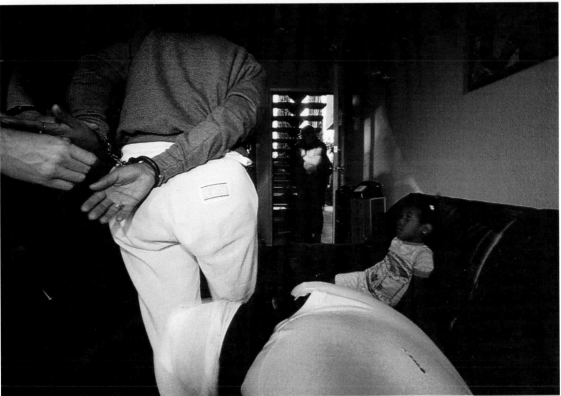

9031
Paolini also made a reportage on juvenile delinquents in Los Angeles. In the southern Californian metropolis police are quick with handcuffs and search warrants. A wrong move, the suspicion of drugs possession or the inability to speak English are often enough for an arrest or a house search.

(starts on previous
pages)
**HONOURABLE
MENTION
STORIES**

ANTHONY SUAU
Black Star,
New York, USA,
for Life
9032

9032

A wide-ranging reportage about religious rites performed by Catholics all over Europe. The photographer set out to capture the timelessness of what may look like fanaticism, but what he perceives to be the universal search for a miracle.
Previous pages and facing page: In Seville, hooded figures bearing crosses do penance during Holy Week. At El Rocío, also in Spain, worshippers surge forward to touch a statue of the Virgin. On the island of Tinos, Greece, a woman crawls on hands and knees towards a hilltop church.
This page: A woman makes her way around the stations of the cross wearing a crown of thorns in southern Poland, and a priest hears confession at a local church. On a remote island off the coast of Ireland barefoot Catholics worship in the rain.

**HONOURABLE
MENTION
STORIES**

APRIL SAUL
Philadelphia
Inquirer,
Philadelphia, USA
9033

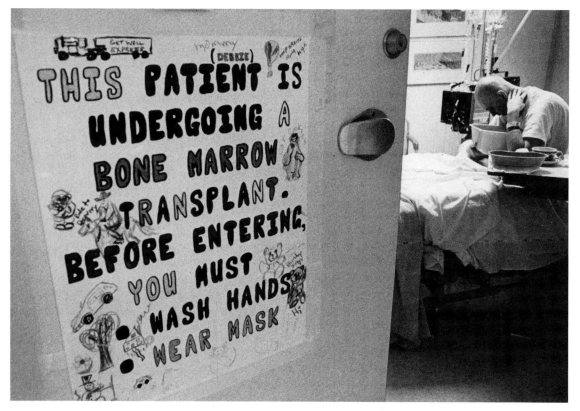

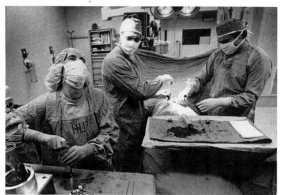

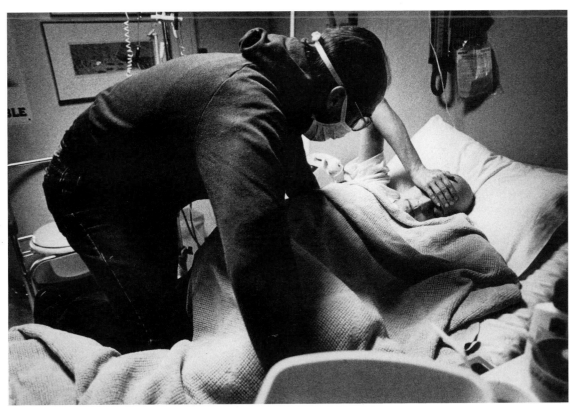

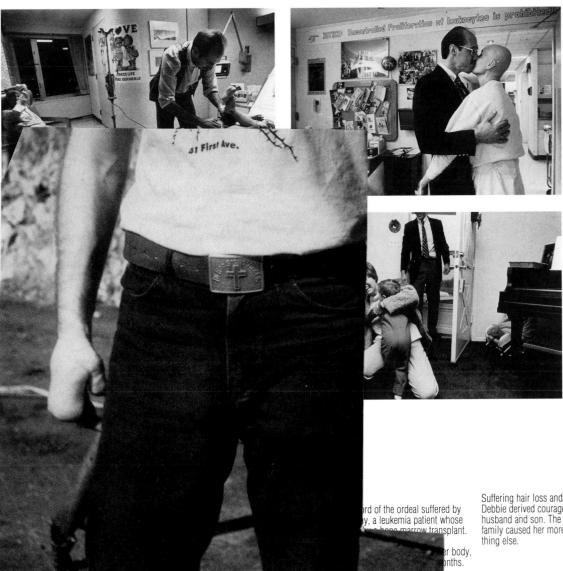

...rd of the ordeal suffered by
...y, a leukemia patient whose
...bone marrow transplant.

...r body,
...nths.

Suffering hair loss and constant nausea,
Debbie derived courage from the visits of her
husband and son. The separation from her
family caused her more anxiety than anything else.

**HONOURABLE
MENTION
SINGLES**

**THOMAS
HEGENBART**
Stern,
Hamburg, FRG
9034

9034
On the way to a new Namibia. A young woman from the Ovahimba tribe takes her children shopping in a supermarket in Opuvo, in the north-west of the country. A harmonious blend of traditional and modern lifestyles.

9035
In the backstreets of Santiago, the Chilean capital, homeless kids keep themselves amused by mimicking their favourite singers. They are known as *cartoneros* because a cardboard box is often all that shields them from the elements.

**HONOURABLE
MENTION
SINGLES**

KARIM DAHER
Gamma,
Paris, France
9036

9036
Violence continued to dominate life in Beirut
in 1989. While smoke billows from the
burning Dora oil refinery in the background,
an engineer checks a telephone connection.
Amazingly, it works.

**THIRD PRIZE
STORIES**

**ANATOLY
IOLIS**
Moscow, USSR
9037

9037
Picture stories about young criminals and the way the law deals with them scored highly in this category. This reportage, submitted by a Russian freelance photographer, illustrates the daily routine in a Soviet prison camp for female offenders.

**FIRST PRIZE
STORIES**

**MIGUEL
FAIRBANKS**
Santa Cruz, USA
9038

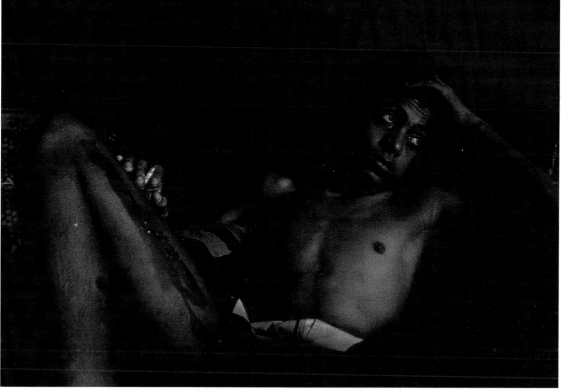

9038
The sad tale of Joabe Pereira da Silva, nick-named McDonald because that's where he once worked. In Baixada Fluminense, a Rio de Janeiro slum, he lives in an environment of desperate poverty and rampant crime. McDonald and his friends practise the suici-dal sport of train surfing, which cost 144 youths their lives in one year. At top, he crouches under 3,300 volt cables while moving at 100 km/hour, and tempts fate hanging on to a train at night. The *surfista* initiation rites involve dressing up in drag (bottom left). Above, McDonald nurses a self-inflicted bullet wound in the small room he shares with his mother and brother (overleaf).

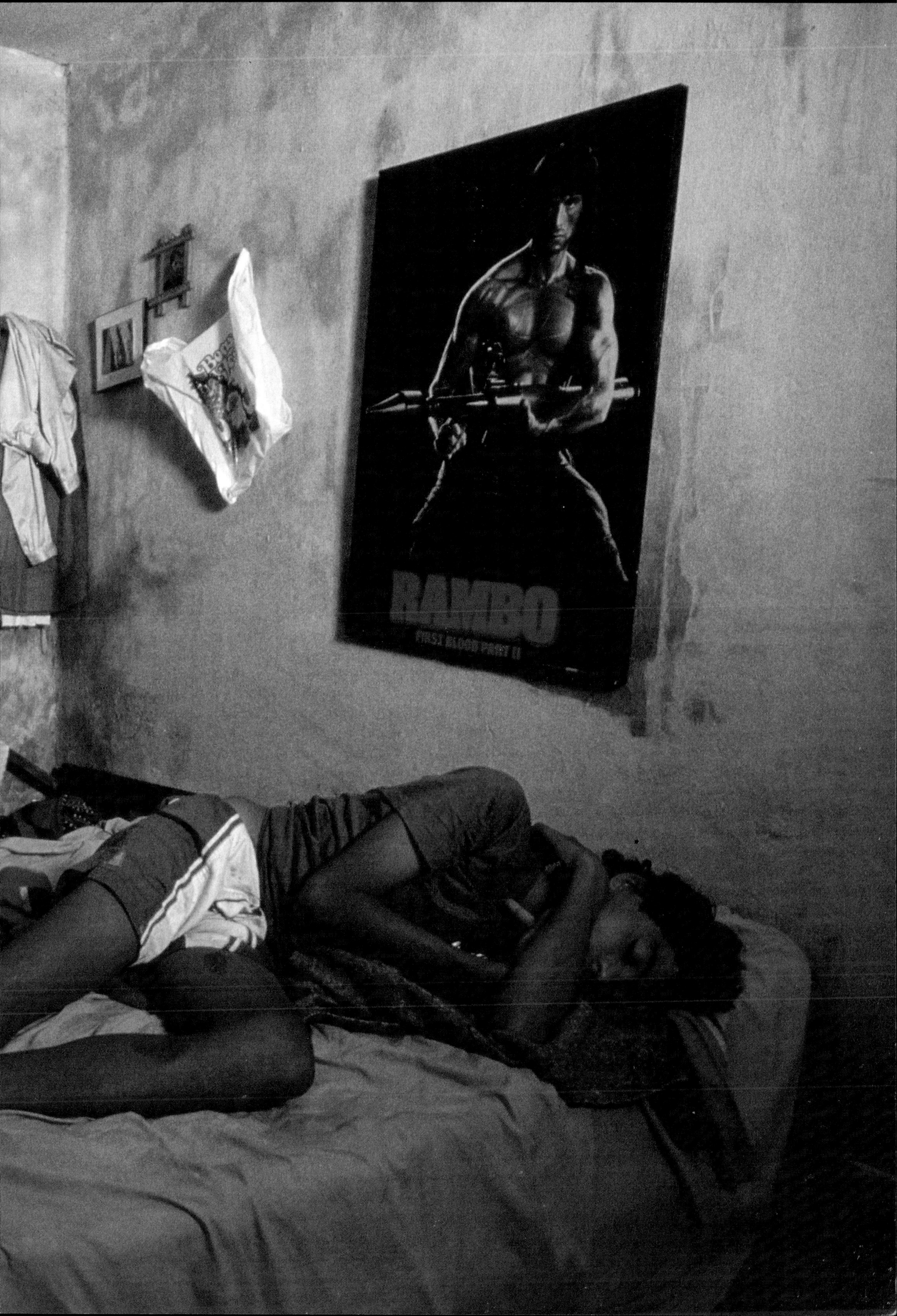
RAMBO
FIRST BLOOD PART II

**THIRD PRIZE
SINGLES**

GERD LUDWIG
Fortune,
New York, USA
9039

GERD LUDWIG
Fortune,
New York, USA
9040

9039
In North American cities the number of black fathers who shirk their responsibilities is stunning, but there are exceptions. Here teenage fathers attend a workshop designed to teach them how to deal with their offspring.

9040
Part of Ludwig's photo essay on *The Black Urban Man* was shot at the Cook County Department of Corrections in Chicago. A young offender peers out from his cell as a prison warden stands guard.

**FIRST PRIZE
SINGLES**

IVAN KURTOV
TASS,
Moscow, USSR
9041

**SECOND PRIZE
SINGLES**

JAMES KAMP
Black Star,
New York, USA,
for Life
9042

9041
On V-Day Anatoly Golimbievsky, a heavily decorated veteran who lost both legs in the Second World War, acknowledges the salute of four young sailors. They were pictured in Leningrad, which was given the title City of Heroes after the war.

9042
Five-year-old Jennifer Royal gives evidence in a Miami courtroom. In a drugs-related shooting in Liberty City, Florida, she had been a witness to the murder of her best friend, Peaches.

**FIRST PRIZE
SINGLES**

**GERARD
VANDYSTADT**
Vandystadt,
Paris, France
9043

9043
An inscrutable jury follows the performance
of low-flying Chinese gymnast Wang Xiuyun
at the 15th International Gymnastics
Tournament at Corbeil near Paris. The
tournament was held in May.

**YANN
GUICHAOUA**
Vandystadt,
Paris, France
9044

9044
A balancing act by Boris Becker at the French
Open Tennis Championships. Seventeen-
year-old American newcomer Michael Chang
became the youngest ever men's champion
at Roland Garros, but a month later Becker
took the title at Wimbledon.

THIRD PRIZE
SINGLES

TIM CLAYTON
Yorkshire Post,
Leeds, UK
9045

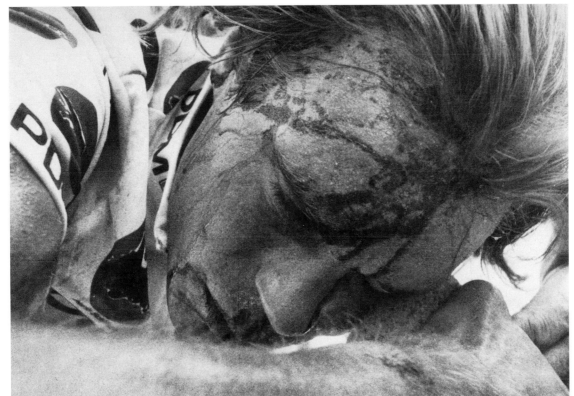

KLAAS-JAN
VAN DER WEIJ
Weesp,
the Netherlands
9046

9045
It's easy to see why the photographer called this picture *Breath-stroke*. Olympic swimmer James Parrack heads for the surface during training for the Commonwealth Games. He took the silver medal in the 100 metres... breast-stroke.

9046
Dutch speed cyclist Gert-Jan Theunisse bites the dust in the 12th stage of the 1989 Tour de France. He got his revenge later by arriving first at Alpe d'Huez and coming fourth in the final classification.

YANN GUICHAOUA
Vandystadt,
Paris, France
9047

RALF STOCKHOFF
GES,
Karlsruhe, FRG
9048

9047
Laurent Fignon heads his team during a time trial in Luxembourg at the beginning of the Tour de France. The 3,232-kilometre race ended with the French champion being beaten by American Greg LeMond by the smallest ever margin of eight seconds.

9048
The red gravel of Roland Garros colours the costume of tennis player Aranxtha Sanchez, the surprise winner of the Paris Open. In the women's final the Spanish girl beat favourite Steffi Graf in three sets.

**SECOND PRIZE
SINGLES**

SIMON BRUTY
Allsport,
London, UK
9049

9049
Captain Atsushi Ogagi pays the price of possession during a rugby match between the
universities of Cambridge and Dashisha,
Japan. At Cambridge's Grange Road ground
the English team beat their visitors 23-19.

**FIRST PRIZE
SINGLES**

**NORBERT
ROSING**
Silvestris,
Kastl, FRG
9050

9050
Bird's-eye view. This German bird-watcher
was the victim of a two-pronged attack. After
his hat and anorak had been soiled by
seagull droppings, he found himself
confronted with a beady eye.

9051
At the Trappist monastery in Tilburg in the
southern Netherlands life isn't *all* austerity.
For the young monk at the top a parental visit
is a cheerful occasion. A few drinks and a
game of cards are permitted on religious
holidays, and the working day ends with a
glass of home brew.

SECOND PRIZE
SINGLES

JIM MONE
Associated Press,
New York, USA
9052

9052
On his way home a week after undergoing
skull surgery, former US President Reagan
exposes a partly shaven head as he doffs his
baseball cap to well-wishers. Nancy Reagan
tries to cover up her husband's weak spot
from behind.

**FIRST PRIZE
STORIES**

**THIRD PRIZE
SINGLES**

**FRANS MARTEN
LANTING**
National Geographic,
Washington DC, USA
9053

9053
South Georgia, a remote British island in the
Antarctic, was the location for this picture
story (continued overleaf), which won three
different prizes. Above, a colony of king
penguins is gathered on a glacier against a
majestic polar backdrop.

9053 (continued)
Top: A wandering albatross displays his
mighty wing-span. Above right, his grey-
headed cousins perform their courtship
ritual, and a giant petrel is shown nesting in
the snow.

**FIRST PRIZE
SINGLES**

**FRANS MARTEN
LANTING**
National Geographic,
Washington DC,
USA
9053

Top: An elephant seal appears to cry out in
agony as he is drowning in mud. Many seals
die in this way every year, but this one was
lucky: the photographer managed to pull him
clear. A giant petrel (right) scavenges on a
seal carcass. Left: A seal pup in an appealing
pose.

SECOND PRIZE
STORIES

OLIVIER FÖLLMI
Genève,
Switzerland
9054

9054

For eight months per year the village of Zanskar, in the heart of the Himalayas, is cut off from the outside world. Only when temperatures drop to -30° C is a path created: a frozen river at the bottom of a canyon, which if all goes well enables the villagers to reach Ladakh, the nearest town, in about 12 days.

In May an expedition was mounted by some adults and two children, who had to be enrolled at the school in Ladakh. Snow-storms (facing page, right) reduce visibility, making progress painfully slow. The children, 12-year-old Motup and his sister Diskit, 9 (above), are experts at testing the ice with their sticks.

**THIRD PRIZE
STORIES**

RON SANFORD
Black Star,
New York, USA
9055

9055
At Brooks Falls in Katmai National Park,
Alaska, a brown bear teaches his cubs to fish
for salmon. Direct eye contact between adult
bears (centre left) spells trouble. A struggle
over fishing rights ensues.

HONOURABLE
MENTION
STORIES

IGOR KOSTIN
Novosti,
Moscow, USSR
9056

9056
Today face masks are widely used in the
Narodichi district in the Ukraine, 80
kilometres from Chernobyl. It wasn't until 40
months after the nuclear disaster that the
Soviet government decided to partly evacuate
the area. In that time 190 mutants had been
born in the contaminated villages.

SECOND PRIZE
SINGLES

ERIC MENCHER
Philadelphia
Inquirer,
Philadelphia, USA
9057

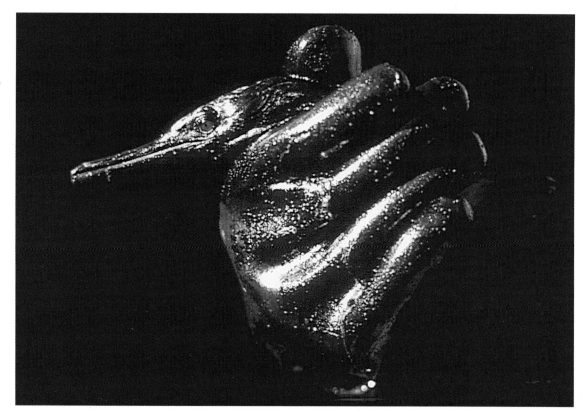

CHILDREN'S
PRESS PHOTO OF
THE YEAR

ROSEMARY KAUL
Los Angeles Times,
Los Angeles, USA
9058

9057
Crude insult to nature. The gloved hand of a rescue worker cradles an oil-soaked victim of the supertanker Exxon Valdez, which struck a reef and burst open on March 24. Eleven million gallons of oil poured into Alaska's Prince William Sound.

9058
Another feathered victim of the ecological nightmare triggered by the Exxon Valdez. This helpless bird, stranded on the rocks of Seal Island, Alaska, won the votes of the Children's Jury. About 1,000 miles of coastline was fouled by the oil spill.

JAMES BALOG
Black Star,
New York, USA
9059

9059
These portraits of a panda, a Florida panther,
a red kangaroo and an Asian elephant are
taken from a series of ten endangered
species, submitted under the title *Survivors*.
The way they are portrayed is intended to be
read as a metaphor for their condition, cut off
as they are from their natural environment.

**SECOND PRIZE
STORIES**

EMILE LUIDER
Rapho,
Paris, France
9060

9060
In Paris the La Villette science park has been
created on the site of a slaughterhouse . The
Museum of Science and Industry is
especially popular with the younger
generation. Here a group of children are
watching a three-dimensional film about
marine life, which is so realistic that they are
trying to catch the fish (continued overleaf).

9060 (continued)
Above: The futuristic effect of the Géode on a moonlit night, and an audience captivated by composite images at the planetarium. Facing page: Trompe-l'oeil effects and other soap bubbles.

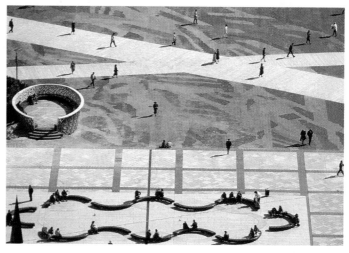

**FIRST PRIZE
STORIES**

EMILE LUIDER
Rapho,
Paris, France
9061

9061
In the year the Eiffel Tower celebrated its centenary, Paris unveiled a new symbol of modern technology: the Grande Arche de la Défense. Designed by Danish architect Otto von Spreckelsen, its completion coincided with the bicentennial of the French revolution in July. This series shows different aspects of La Défense, Paris' new business district, pictured while the arch was under construction. The creative approach of the city planners is borne out by the use of sculpture by artists such as Takis (far left) and Calder (above).

**SECOND PRIZE
STORIES**

NATALIE FOBES
National Geographic,
Washington DC, USA
9062

9062
In March the worst oil disaster in the history of the United States made headlines all over the world. For the population of Alaska, both animal and human, Good Friday became very bad indeed when the Exxon Valdez ran aground. An area the size of New Jersey in Prince William Sound was covered with a thick blanket of oil and 1,000 miles of the state's rocky coast became badly contaminated. An army of workers was mobilised to clean up the coastline (continued overleaf).

9062 (continued)
From top: Perched on Bligh Reef, the Exxon Valdez continues to disgorge oil. Five days after the accident the layer of oil floating on the water had in places become 45 centimetres thick. A dog-tired crew of cleaners returns after a 12-hour shift, but their work cannot stop native Alaskan Sonya Knight weeping for the casualties of this 20th-century version of the Black Death. More than 1,000 sea otters and about 240,000 birds were killed by the oil spill. Facing page: A common murre beats its wings in a futile attempt to fly away.

THIRD PRIZE
STORIES

FIRST PRIZE
SINGLES
(overleaf)

ERIC BOUVET
Gamma,
Paris, France
9063

9063
The Ayatollah Khomeini, leader of the Islamic Republic of Iran and an inspiration to fundamentalists and terrorists, died at the age of 89. The death sentence he had passed on British author Salman Rushdie was not carried out during his lifetime.

Mass hysteria and utter chaos reigned in the streets of Tehran as the funeral cortège made its way to the grave. Among the millions of mourners giving free rein to their grief, several people were crushed to death; many more fainted and suffered injuries. After July's presidential elections Rafsanjani (above left) emerged as Iran's new leader (continued overleaf).

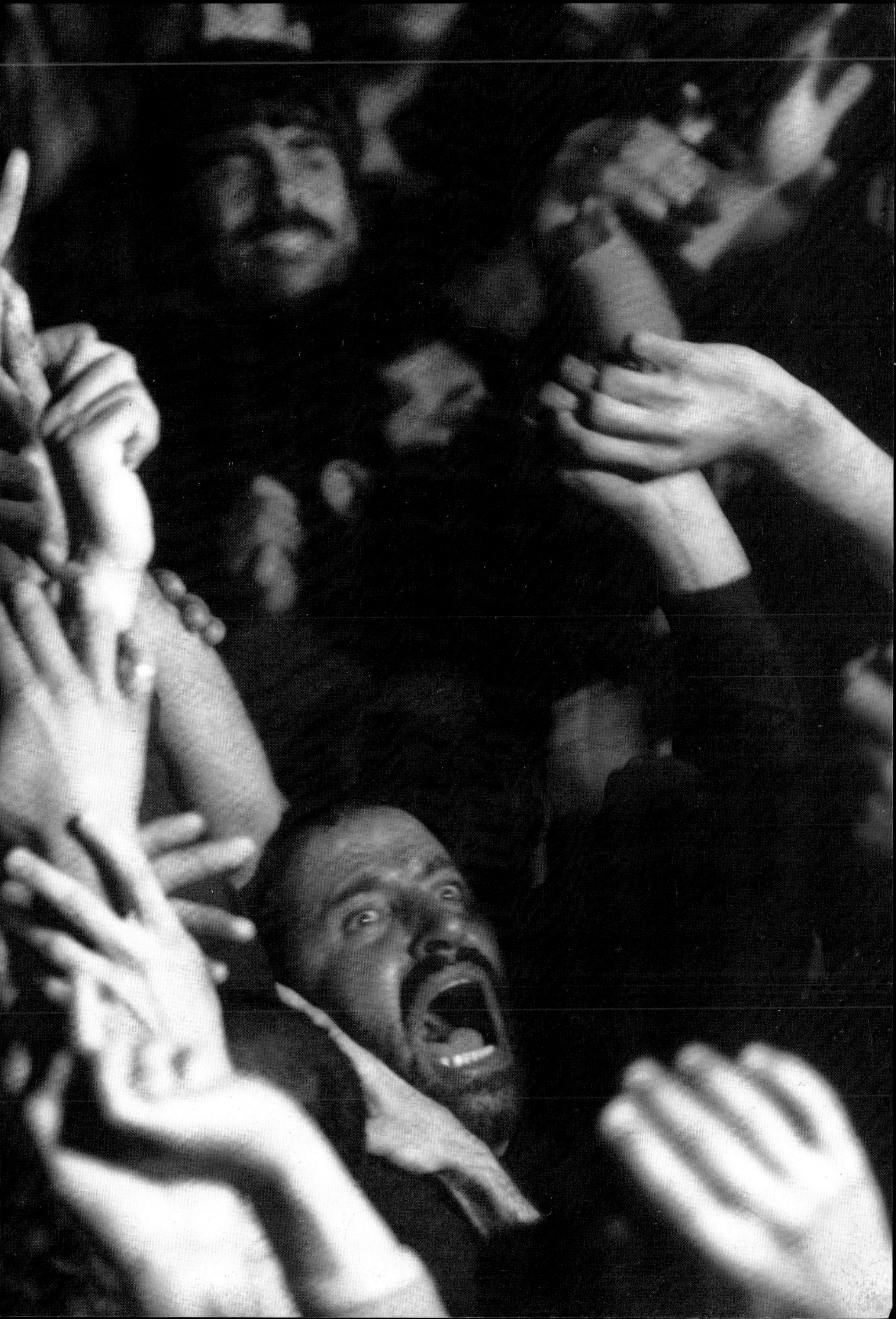

JOAN WAKELIN
Reading, UK
9064

9064
Conditions are dire for the Vietnamese boat people living in overcrowded refugee camps in Hong Kong. Stacked up in multi-tiered bunk-beds and even cages (top), the 57,000 refugees who have made it to the Crown Colony live in hope of a better future. Shot at the 'closed centres' of Sham Shui Po in Kowloon and (far left) Pillar Point in the New Territories, this reportage was made 11 months before 51 Vietnamese refugees were rounded up at dawn and repatriated. The British government defended itself against the international outcry which followed by saying that tension in the camps was becoming unbearable.

**HONOURABLE
MENTION
SINGLES**

**LIU HEUNG
SHING**
Associated Press,
New York, USA
9065

9065
Not realising that the army surveys the scene
from above, a young Chinese couple hesitate
to leave the relative protection of an
underpass in Beijing. The picture was taken
when the authorities were reasserting their
control of the country in early June.

PETER TURNLEY
Black Star,
New York, USA,
for Newsweek
9066

**HONOURABLE
MENTION
SINGLES**

**KENNETH
JARECKE**
Contact Press Images,
New York, USA,
for Time
9067

9066
The lull after the storm. A golden sunset sets Tiananmen Square aglow, silhouetting the Goddess of Democracy against the sky. A few days later the Chinese counterpart of the Statue of Liberty lay in pieces.

9067
Both sides of the conflict. Soldiers of the People's Liberation Army guarding Zhongnanhai, Beijing's seat of power, face a solitary symbol of the struggle for democracy: a student on hunger strike.

RITA REED
Minneapolis
Star Tribune,
Minneapolis, USA
9068

9068
In 1989 the US government made a
determined effort to stem the flow of Bolivian
cocaine by attacking the problem at its
source. In Operation Snowcap various US
authorities joined forces with Umopar,
Bolivia's police force. They focussed their
attention on Chapare Valley, Cocaine Alley to
the Americans.

Caught red-handed, Eugenio Quispe (facing page, top and right) is forced to slit the sides of his fabrica and watch the product of a long night's work gush away. Umopar officers are the only ones authorised to destroy the cocaine, but first the powder is carefully weighed and recorded.

This page, from top: plainclothes US agents ensure control of the valley's cocaine capital while prisoners are marched out of town. As the townspeople watch incredulously, American Bruce Norum vents his anger on their livelihood. The two tons of cocaine confiscated in this raid represent a wholesale value in the US of $14.2 million.

**SECOND PRIZE
SINGLES**

**EDVARD
ETTINGER**
Ogonyok,
Moscow, USSR
9069

CAROL GUZY
The Washington Post,
Washington DC, USA
9070

9069
July saw the first ever nationwide strikes in the Soviet Union. Although miners are relatively well paid, the strike spread rapidly from Siberia to other parts of the country. When half a million miners, representing 40 per cent of Soviet coal production, had downed tools, most of their demands were met.

9070
Reviving the 1968 dream that turned into a nightmare, change came to Czechoslovakia in 1989. Here a jubilant young man occupies an abandoned guard tower near Devin, on the border between Czechoslovakia and Austria.

CRAIG FUJII
The Seattle Times,
Seattle, USA
9071

DIANA WALKER
Time,
New York, USA
9072

9071
Sea lions seek sanctuary on a buoy marking the traffic lanes in Prince William Sound, Alaska. The Exxon Valdez, the supertanker that caused a major ecological disaster in March, is perched atop Bligh Reef in the background.

9072
Aboard the *Maksim Gorky*, a Russian cruise ship anchored off the island of Malta, Mikhail Gorbachev and George Bush met in December for an informal summit. The success of the meeting was illustrated by the fact that the two world leaders gave a joint press conference. 'He is a guy quite sure of what he's doing,' said Bush of his Soviet counterpart.

**FIRST PRIZE
STORIES**

**ANDREI
SOLOVIEV**
TASS,
Moscow, USSR
9073

ДА ЗДРАВСТВУЕТ
МАРКСИЗМ-ЛЕНИНИЗМ
-ВЕЧНО ЖИВОЕ
РЕВОЛЮЦИОННОЕ
ИНТЕРНАЦИОНАЛЬНОЕ
УЧЕНИЕ !

9073

As nationalists all over the Soviet Union clamoured for autonomy, ethnic strife hit many of the outlying republics where some 140 million non-Russians live. Facing page: In Baku, Azerbaijan, 100,000 demonstrators gathered at the foot of Lenin's statue. Under the watchful eye of the old communist heroes a mass rally was held in Nagorno Karabakh (top and overleaf), and in May political unrest claimed victims among the Turkish population of Uzbekistan (above).

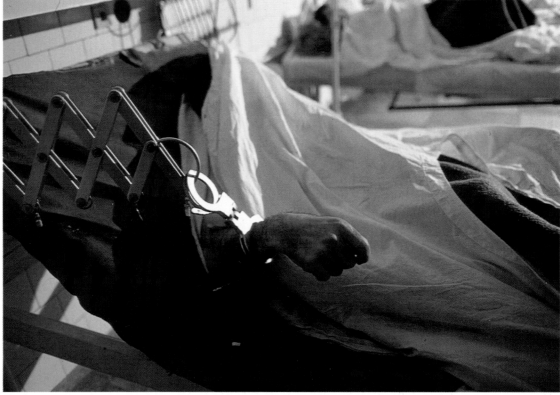

9074
A moment's respite in the streets of
Bucharest. During the eventful days of
December Romanian soldiers interrupt their
battle with the Securitate secret police to
share a bite to eat. Whenever the fighting
lessened, citizens flooded into the street.

9075
You can't be too careful. In a Bucharest
hospital a member of Ceaucescu's well-
equipped, 180,000-strong Securitate lies
devoid of life, but still handcuffed to his bed.
Of all Warsaw Pact party leaders, Ceausescu
was the only one who tried to stop change by
resorting to large-scale violence.

**THIRD PRIZE
SINGLES**

DAVID TURNLEY
Black Star,
New York, USA,
for Detroit
Free Press
9076

9076
In May and June the winner of last year's
Premier Award was to be found in Beijing. As
the pro-democracy movement gained
momentum it spread from the universities to
other population groups. Here a woman
pleads with soldiers in a convoy sent to the
capital to quench the uprising.